Animal Homes

Bees and Their Hives

by Linda Tagliaferro

Consulting Editor: Gail Saunders-Smith, Ph.D.

Consultant: Gary A. Dunn, Director of Education
Young Entomologists' Society
Lansing, Michigan

Capstone press

Mankato, Minnesota

Building the Hive

Bees live in hives. Bees build
hives in trees or logs.

Bees work for about

two weeks to make a hive.

Bees use wax to build hives. Bees make the wax inside their bodies.

9

Inside the Hive

Bees shape wax into cells.

Rows of wax cells make

a honeycomb.

A queen bee lays thousands
of eggs. She lays one egg
in each cell.

queen bee →

Young bees hatch from
the eggs. Worker bees
feed the young bees.

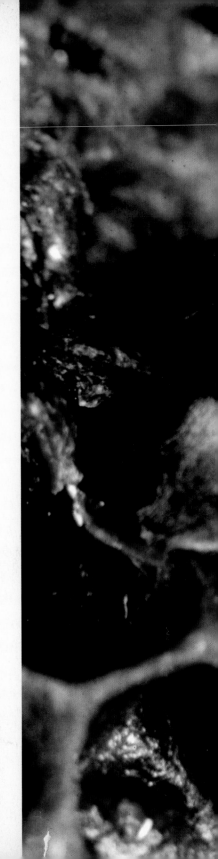

Guard bees protect the hive.
They sting enemies that try
to come inside the hive.

honeybee guarding box hive ➤

In hot weather, bees quickly
fan their wings. Fanning
cools the hive.

A Good Home

Bees buzz and fly into their hives. Hives are good homes for bees.

honeybees entering box hive ➡

Glossary

cell—a small section in the honeycomb of a hive; cells have six sides.

enemy—a person or animal that wants to harm or destroy another person or animal

hive—a structure where a colony of bees live; thousands of bees live in one hive.

honeycomb—a group of wax cells built by worker bees inside their hives; bees store pollen, nectar, honey, and eggs in the cells of a honeycomb.

protect—to guard or keep safe from harm

queen bee—an adult female bee that lays eggs; only one queen bee lives in a hive.

sting—to poke with a small sharp point

worker bee—an adult female bee that does not lay eggs; worker bees build hives and take care of young bees.

Read More

Penny, Malcolm. *Bees.* The Secret World Of. Chicago: Raintree, 2004.

Spilsbury, Louise. *A Colony of Bees.* Animal Groups. Chicago: Heinemann Library, 2004.

Trumbauer, Lisa. *The Life Cycle of a Bee.* Life Cycles. Mankato, Minn.: Pebble Books, 2003.

Internet Sites

FactHound offers a safe, fun way to find Internet sites related to this book. All of the sites on FactHound have been researched by our staff.

Here's how:

1. Visit *www.facthound.com*

2. Type in this special code **0736823824** for age-appropriate sites. Or enter a search word related to this book for a more general search.

3. Click on the **Fetch It** button.

FactHound will fetch the best sites for you!

Index/Word List